Pebble® Plus

LET'S LOOK AT
GERMANY

BY MARY BOONE

raintree
a Capstone company — publishers for children

Raintree is an imprint of Capstone Global Library Limited, a company incorporated in England and Wales having its registered office at 264 Banbury Road, Oxford, OX2 7DY – Registered company number: 6695582

www.raintree.co.uk
myorders@raintree.co.uk

Edited by Jessica Server
Designed by Juliette Peters
Picture research by Jo Miller
Production by Laura Manthe
Originated by Capstone Global Library Ltd
Printed and bound in India

ISBN 978 1 4747 8449 8 (hardback)
ISBN 978 1 4747 8466 5 (paperback)

British Library Cataloguing in Publication Data
A full catalogue record for this book is available from the British Library.

Photo Credits
Alamy: dpa picture alliance archive, 17; Shutterstock: A.N.Foto, 2-3, canadastock, Cover Bottom, Cover Back, 21, 22-23, 24, cornfield, 12-13, FooTToo, 15, Globe Turner, 22 (Inset), Juergen Wackenhut, 6-7, Max Topchil, Cover Middle, nale, 4 (map), Oleg Golovnev, 16, Ondrej Deml, 9, PhotoLondonUK, Cover Top, RockerStocker, 18-19, S-F, 14, S.Borisov, 1, Sharkshock, 10-11, YoPho, 4-5

Every effort has been made to contact copyright holders of material reproduced in this book. Any omissions will be rectified in subsequent printings if notice is given to the publisher.

All the internet addresses (URLs) given in this book were valid at the time of going to press. However, due to the dynamic nature of the internet, some addresses may have changed, or sites may have changed or ceased to exist since publication. While the author and publisher regret any inconvenience this may cause readers, no responsibility for any such changes can be accepted by either the author or the publisher.

CONTENTS

Where is Germany?

Germany is a country in Europe. It is one and a half times larger than the United Kingdom.

Its capital city is Berlin.

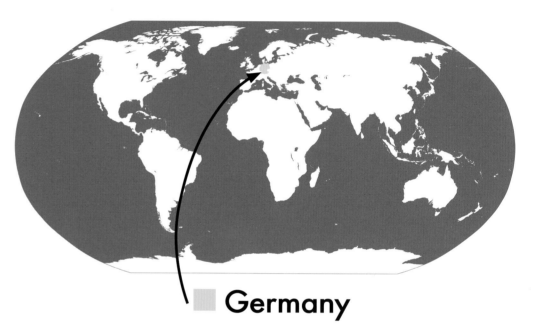

Germany

Berlin

From forests to mountains

The Black Forest is in Germany's south-west. The Bavarian Alps are there too. They are made up of many mountain ranges. The North German Plain has marshes and rivers.

Black Forest

In the wild

Many animals live in Germany. Wild goats called ibex live in the mountains. Wildcats roam the forests. Golden eagles can be seen flying in the sky above.

ibex

People

German tribes lived in Germany thousands of years ago. Many people have come to live in Germany from Turkey, Poland and Italy. Germany is a popular place for immigrants today.

At the table

Sausages made of pork or beef are popular in Germany. These sausages are called wursts. Potato and cabbage are common German foods. Germans also bake tasty breads.

Festivals

Oktoberfest is Germany's most famous festival. People gather in the city of Munich to eat, drink and listen to music. Many people wear traditional costumes.

At work

Many Germans have jobs making machines or food. Some make cars in cities. In the country, farmers grow grains and raise animals.

Transport

Germany's motorway system is called the autobahn. Many people in large cities get around by train or bus. Some people travel on trams.

train

Famous place

Neuschwanstein Castle is a famous castle in Germany. People began building it in 1869. It sits on a cliff in the Bavarian Alps. More than 1 million people visit it each year.

QUICK GERMANY FACTS

Germany's flag

Name: Germany

Capital: Berlin

Other major cities: Hamburg, Munich, Cologne, Frankfurt

Population: 80,457,737 (July 2018 estimate)

Size: 357,387 sq km (137,988 square miles)

Language: German

Money: euro

GLOSSARY

capital   the city in a country where the government is based

famous   known about by many people

immigrant   a person who comes to live permanently in a foreign country

marsh   an area of wet, low land usually covered in grasses and low plants

pork   the meat from pigs

traditional   something passed down through time

tram   a public transportation vehicle that moves on overhead rails

tribe   a group of people who share the same language and way of life

FIND OUT MORE

Books

Europe (Introducing Continents), Chris Oxlade and Anita Ganeri (Raintree, 2018)

Germany (Country Guides with Benjamin Blog), Anita Ganeri (Raintree, 2014)

Germany Unpacked, Clive Gifford (Wayland, 2017)

Websites

Find more facts and details about Germany at these great websites.

www.kids-world-travel-guide.com/germany-facts.html

www.natgeokids.com/uk/discover/geography/countries/country-fact-file-germany/

www.sciencekids.co.nz/sciencefacts/countries/germany.html

COMPREHENSION QUESTIONS

1. Germany has different types of transport. Which one would you like to try? Why?

2. Germany has a famous festival called Oktoberfest. What do people do at Oktoberfest?

3. What animal can be found living in the mountains in Germany?

INDEX